Terrestrial Music

Terrestrial Music

poems by

John Bradley

Curbstone Press

First Edition: 2006

printed in U.S. on acid-free paper
Cover design: Stone Graphics

This book was published with the support of the
Connecticut Commission on Culture and Tourism, the
National Endowment for the Arts, the State of
Connecticut Office of Policy and Management, and
donations from many individuals. We are very
grateful for this support.

Many thanks to Jane Blanshard for her help in editing this book.

Library of Congress Cataloging-in-Publication Data

Bradley, John, 1950-
    Terrestrial music / by John Bradley. -- 1st ed.
        p. cm.
    ISBN-13: 978-1-931896-28-3 (pbk. : acid-free paper)
    ISBN-10: 1-931896-28-3 (pbk. : acid-free paper)
    I. Title.
    PS3602.R3427T47 2006
    811'.6--dc22

                                        2006017587

published by
    CURBSTONE PRESS   321 Jackson St. Willimantic, CT 06226
        phone: 860-423-5110   e-mail: info@curbstone.org
                    www.curbstone.org

Acknowledgments

I wish to thank the editors of the following publications: *Another Chicago Magazine*: "After Viewing the Queen of Outer Space" (1958). *Arsenic Lobster*: "I Sing the Body Atomic." *Atomic Ghost: Poets Respond to the Nuclear Age* (Coffee House Press): "Sailors Shielding Their Eyes During Atomic Bomb Test, Bikini, 1947." *Barnabe Mountain Review*: "Story with Blue and Green." *Beyond Lament: Poets of the World Bearing Witness to the Holocaust* (Northwestern Univ. Press): "Letter to Dina." *Blue Mesa Review*: "After Viewing The Queen of Outer Space (1958)." *Bluff City*: "After a Rain." *CQ*: "Terrestrial Music/2." *Calapooya Collage*: "Escalation." *Cincinnati Poetry Review*: "Sailors Shielding Their Eyes During Atomic Bomb Test, Bikini, 1947." *Clackamas Literary Review*: "Jesus and the Corn Mothers." *College English*: "Cocoon" and "Where I Live." *Germination* (Canada): "Insomnia of the News." Goshen College Broadside Series: "Story with Blue and Green." *Heartlands Today: The Real Work*: "Terrestrial Music," and "How Shall We Tell Each Other of the Poet?" *The Life and Writing of Muriel Rukeyser* (St. Martin's Press): "The Uses of Poetry." *In the West of Ireland: A Literary Celebration* (Enright House): "To Dance with Uranium," *Kerf*: "Bosnian Love Poem," "Earth Angel," and "White Footprints." *Luna*: "On the Death of Pol Pot" and "Reckoning." *The Mid-America Poetry Review:* "The Angels of Sodom." *Milkwood Review*: "Improper Disposal." *Like Thunder: Poets Respond to the Violence in America* (Univ. of Iowa Press): "Improper Disposal." *New Voices: Poetry and Fiction from Colorado State University* (Center for Literary Publishing): "Letter to Dina." *Pacific Coast Journal*: "Involving the Use of the Word America." *Pavement Saw*: "Unforgiven H20." *Pemmican*: "Radithor: A Short History in Four Reels," "Science as a Mechanism of Exclusion," and "Watch Alice Glow." *The Plaza* (Japan): "Where I Live." *The Prose Poem: An International Journal*: "Mortal Colors with a Commentary." *Red Dirt*: "Animal Light." *Rockhurst Review*: "Mortal Colors." *Sundog*: "Letter to Dina." *This*: "On Hearing the Voice of Walt Whitman." *Tonatzin*: "Vice President Quayle's Visit with General Pinochet, March 1990." *Towers*: "The Institute of Nuclear Poetics" and "The Uses of Poetry." *Winners: A Retrospective of the Washington Prize* (Word Works): "On the Death of Pol Pot" and "The Uses of Poetry." *WPFW Poetry Anthology* (Bunny and Crocodile Press): "After a Rain."

Some of the poems in this manuscript have appeared in the following chapbooks: *The New Wine Dreaming in the Vat* (Mesilla Press), *To Dance with Uranium* (Lake Effect Press), *Pilgrimage to a Gingko Tree* (World Friendship Center), and *Add Musk Here* (Pavement Saw Press). Blessings upon all their houses.

It takes a village to raise a poem. A special thanks to all those who provided terrestrial (and extraterrestrial) encouragement for these poems, especially Ric and Bonnie Amesquita, Beth Bentley and Ed Dougherty, Pat and Dave Brodsky, Allan Cooper, Bob Edwards, Martín Espada, Joe Gastiger, Ray Gonzalez, Jim Grabill, Christine Holloway, Kent Johnson, George Kalamaras, Ken Letko, Becky Parfitt, Susan Porterfield, Ryan Van Cleave, Terry Tempest Williams, Bill Witherup, and Phil Woods. And most of all, to Jana.

For Jana
Jesse and Laurie
Mom and Joan
Dad and Dan

and all other terrestrials

"Pardon me, if when I want
to tell the story of my life
it's the land I talk about.
This is the land.
It grows in your blood
and you grow.
If it dies in your blood
you die out."

—Pablo Neruda,
translated by William O'Daly

Contents

Terrestrial Music

WHERE I LIVE

Where I Live

I live on the corner
of Ninth and Lewis, the last
house on the last corner
of the last block. I live

in that house where moss
and morning glories conspire
to topple the porch. I live

in that slab of light
you see suspended
in the night. Once inside
I'm no different

than any other
visitor to any other
star. That's what I love

about this story.

Terrestrial Music

Dirt underneath
     my fingernails, sweat
   stinging my eyes.
All I want
    before I die is
  to bite into
sun-warm tomato.

         *

     What did I find
   in spade-loosened soil?
Coal cinder clothespin
     spring
   beer cap plastic Indian
with head bitten
    off in mulch sleep.

         *

   The old man who's my neighbor,
he says hello
    for the first time.
   So this is what happens
when you kneel
    down and plant
tomatoes.

         *

Watering the seedlings,
   I remember
  my father's words:

"Put supports around them
        while they're still
    little penises."

                *

"A baby"
        the morning
    paper says
"in the back room
        of a church
    the headless corpse
of a baby."
        Go out
    to the garden
breathe the pure
        scent of burning manure.

                *

    What creature dared
nibble the little
        leaves of my baby
    tomato plants?
If terrestrial music
        excited your ears
    tickled your tongue
wouldn't you?

                *

    In the back shed
    on a bed of dead leaves
fingers curled
        curling
    my work gloves rest.
Two empty nests

waiting to hold
something soft
and round
and fallen.

Involving the Use of the Word "America"

"In America," Kafka began, and paused, staring at the peeling gray planks on the front porch. "In America," he began again, but lost his way in the enormity of the phrase.

It was a sticky August day, but Kafka still wore his heavy gray overcoat and black bowler.

"Would you like a beer?" I asked, but he shook his head, pointing to his throat.

"What would you say if the President of the United States came up to your front porch right now?" Kafka asked, trying to be patient, "If he shook your hand and patted you on the back? What would you say?"

"Offer him a beer?"

"Would you tell him how you ate your landlord because he stole your father's eyebrows? Would you tell him how your wife ran off with your uranium which you kept hidden in the valium? Would you tell him Jack Ruby is secretly transmitting coded messages through the letters turned by Vanna White?"

"Probably not."

"No, this is America. You would, instead, ask for parrots, obscenely colored parrots, to be released from cornfields in Nebraska and Iowa and Ohio. Thousands of purple and yellow and green parrots. Isn't that what you really want?"

I shrugged my shoulders. "Sounds all right to me, I guess."

His face looked tight, sallow, like an egg boiled too long. If I took a spoon and broke open the egg, I knew what I would see—garishly colored parrots perched on televisions of all sizes strewn across a cornfield. And, when a parrot opened its beak, out would fly tiny felt parrots wearing black sombreros, with little bandoleers slung across their breasts. I sighed, my breath a sticky purple.

"See?" said Kafka, cleaning his nails with a switchblade, its handle a larger-than-normal sausage. "In America," he began again, losing his way in the enormity of the phrase.

Reckoning

All of us take shelter in the safest place
we know—the basement. Dad, stabbing
his toothpick at a piece of corn stuck
between his back teeth. Mom, with her red
mechanical pencil, improving her vocabulary
with the *Reader's Digest* quiz. My sister, twirling
round and round on her stool, singing quietly
to *Rubber Soul.* My mother orders her
to turn it off. Now. My sister sighs, turns it off,
and then a minute later, as if she had completely
forgotten what had just been said, turns the music
back on. My brother, tongue sticking out the corner
of his mouth, dips his dinky paint brush
into the coffee can my father filled
with tap water, painting his plastic lawnmower.
Sand and pebbles sting the basement windows.
Underneath the ping-pong table, I press my head
to the cold concrete floor. I can hear Saul,
his marooned-on-Mars voice calling out
on his short wave radio: "Coal Cinder.
This is Mobile One. Handlebars melt
the lilacs. Calico snail tows the library.
Ping-pong table roots in the rubble.
Do you read me, Coal Cinder? Over."

The Angels of Sodom

(After a painting by Gustave Moreau)

Above me
    before me
two elongated
    untethered shapes
hushed titanium gray
    gathering
atom by atom
    substance and then
pure intention.
    Not premeditated
malice but
    something harsher
the insomniac opening
    the door to find his lover
rubbing against her
    lover. And when she comes
to bed that night
    she is shoved, again
and again, out
    of the bed once shared.
Why is it
    I think I know
these blurred shapes
    have seen them
hovering above
    a winter Wal-Mart
beings not nearly
    so cold, so certain
in destruction
    as those
small and great
    below.

Two Tangos with the General

1. Vice President Quayle's Visit with General Pinochet, March 1990

> "Long live death with its terrible speed."
> —Vicente Huidobro

The Vice President opens
his hands, and the reporters
come closer. "The General,"
he tells them, "wants democracy."
No one in the room laughs.

Nearby, Pinochet sits erect.
He tilts his head, listening
for the sound of Victor Jara
and Pablo Neruda tunneling
beneath his feet, tearing
at the soil with their teeth.

In the streets of Santiago
the disappeared are still
in the clicking of rosary beads
on a taxi cab windshield,
in the rasp of curlers against
a clear plastic kerchief,

in the vowels that singe
the mouth of the boy who says
to the flower seller, "I want
to eat your flowers."

At the Ministry of Justice
two men scrub a heavy wall,
scrub the handwriting of someone

who walks in her sleep, leaving
each night a "Viva los Muertos."

Now Pinochet rises, and the cameras
feed. The Vice President
and the General embrace, careful
not to bruise each other's flesh.

2. Unforgiven H2O

Leaning over my bed, clad in a red thong panty and H2O bra (with water-filled inner pockets creating the most natural addition to his bustline) was the one and only General Augusto Pinochet. Is he here to seduce me? To recite a Pablo Neruda love poem? To sell me CIA-imported Viagra? To lead me in a prayer for Orlando Letelier, who died in a car bomb Letelier himself planted just to make Pinochet look bad?

How quick I was to judge the General. All he wanted, he quickly explained while adjusting his water-enhanced breasts, was to borrow my flashlight, so he could find the toilet. He apologized in his most sincere, nondictatorial, free-market tone for disturbing me.

"But why the H2O bra, General?" I inquired. Not that I have anything against an organic, non-toxic approach to enhancing your bustline, of course.

"Cara, I've received such terrible press lately I thought I might be considered more, how do you say, more, more venereal . . . "

"Vulnerable?" I asked.

"Yes, yes, yes. Poor dispirited General Pinochet fannying about in lingerie. Do you think it will work? Should I have listened to those damned advisors with their Ph.Ds in Lingerie Studies?"

At this point, he limped away down the hall. I could hear the homuncular grinding of spinal disk against disk, as he muttered, "Oh, the paradoxical effects of Frederick's of Hollywood lingerie on the American public."

On the Death of Pol Pot

"but the thirst for it/goes on enormous"
—"Of Justice," Hilda Morley

If it is true that Pol Pot is dead, then the blushing tulips
blush in the utilitarian rain. Someone forgets to pray

for the bag of cat litter left underneath the grocery cart
in the parking lot. Freshly cleaned pillowcases smell

of a mole and the earth-hole that is also mole. If Pol Pot
is as dead as last winter's wet leaves, tires are not

rotated. Oil not changed. Lawns uncut. The postal carrier
brings the mail for the neighbor to the east to the neighbor

to the west. Images from *The Killing Fields* drift into every
broadcast of every sporting event. If it is true, Pol Pot died

in his bed, his wife and daughter hearing moisture rise
from a damp sheet, mumble, drift off into a passing breeze.

"Rifle Shots Kill Girl, 12, Racing Out of Her Bed"

(Chicago Tribune, July 11, 2000)

Here, in my brick house out in the corn, miles
from where bullets tore
through her walls as she slept,
here, in a cluster of brick homes called Brickville,
an air force officer once lived. He and his fellow dreamers
worked on a drone, a pilotless plane
to deliver wrath from the sky upon the enemy
even as the enemy slept.

Two men, a high-powered rifle, a couple dozen
bullets. A couple dozen holes through the back
of the house. There's a small white coffin, a service
for Tsarina where police and politicians
say all the right things: Emergency
meetings, protecting our children, taking back
the neighborhood. " We can't expect anybody to save us
from us but us," says a minister who has seen
too many coffins.

In a folder, I save articles
on a national missile defense. The military wants missiles
to shoot down incoming nuclear missiles.
Imagine, they like to tell us, an invisible shield across the sky
to protect us at night in our beds.

Imagine, I'd like to tell them, an invisible shield
around each home in Englewood, around the home
of twelve-year-old Tsarina Powell, who liked to iron
her aunt's clothing, wanted to be a doctor, whose smile
a blurred newspaper photo cannot dim. Where
was the shield around her bed?

I file away Tsarina's story
in the folder marked "Violence." What missile
system, what computer network will protect us
from us?

Margot, Otto, Anne, and Edith Frank, Merwedeplein, Amsterdam, May 1941

In February, just before   his photograph
was taken, 389 Jewish   men were deported [Latin *deportare*,
to carry away]   or, if you prefer: "randomly, senselessly,
sadistically"   carried away first to Buchenwald,
then to Mauthausen. Only   one lived
to return to Holland. As it was   later discovered.

In May, at the time   this photograph was taken, Anne
writes to her grandmother: "We're not likely to get
sunburned..." On the last day   of May, the Nazis barred
Jews. "because we can't go   to the swimming pool."
From public beaches, swimming   pools, parks, spas.
To teach the Jews they were   pariahs [Tamil *parai*, drum].

"Fill out the registration   form," said Anne's teacher.
All pupils from Jewish   families must register.
"by the end of the school day."   That was all
there was to it.   "Too bad, but there's nothing..."
Anne did not tell   her grandmother. "to be done."
Otto and Edith Frank, their faces   already dissolving

into corporeal shadow. Margot   stiff, proper, self-
conscious. Anne, her body   flush with
Otto, one foot forward, one   back. At the moment
the photograph. Beneath my   watch. On the back
of the book. By my bed.   Was taken.
That was all. Is all that can be   said.

Bosnian Love Poem

In Memory of Bosko Brckic and Admira Ismic

He was a Serb, she a Muslim.
A Muslim and Serb in love

in the city of Sarajevo.
That's all we need to know.

The Serbs say the Muslims killed them.
The Muslims say the Serbs killed them.

Both sides had agreed to let Bosko and Admira pass
on Wednesday, at 4 pm. On Wednesday, at 4 pm.,

They died, on the Vrbana Bridge.
In the zone not Muslim nor Serb.

Shot at the same time, Bosko
died first, then Admira, holding him.

For six days, no one came near.
For six days, everyone watched.

Bosko, face down. Admira, left
arm across Bosko's back.

He, a Serb, she, a Muslim, embracing.
Everything we need to know.

"Improper Disposal"

The words suggest illegal
dumping of a bloodstained
mattress or mound of toxic soil.
Not a baby, wrapped
in a woman's sweater, left
on the steps of a church
in weather cold enough to freeze
a bottle of wine. Why
would anyone leave
a baby like this? The police
want to speak to the mother
because the father. . . he could be
anyone and no one, a boy
who can't remember where
he left his sperm, or a cloud
of voices in the form of a dove.

"Intrauterine asphyxia"
states the Cook County medical
examiner's office for cause
of death. The baby stillborn
making the mother not a murderer
but a parent who simply wanted
a Christian burial for her child.
Though she's still guilty
of "improper disposal of a body."
"In her own way, she was caring
for her child," notes the pastor
of the church. "That's no sin."
Sin, in a land where one in five
children go to bed hungry,
is something more
common, less newsworthy.

Cocoon

Giggling from the back row. I continue reading the passage from an autobiographical essay by Maya Angelou as I stroll to the back of the room. When I'm at the back, I stop reading, ask the student with the parka on (despite the sweltering artificial heat) a question about Angelou's essay. He looks up, stunned, as if I had just asked him if penguins eat their young. Then I hear it again, the giggling, this time to my left. There aren't any students on this side of the room, just a jumble of coats and bookbags, but a memory begins to stir. This has already happened, surely this has happened before.

Pulling away layers of winter coats, I soon find what I am looking for—two sleeping bag-sized nylon totes, each one quivering with barely suppressed laughter. With a sharp tug I untie the black bow on each sack, tapping twice with my pencil on each rounded shape within as I tell the two students-in-hiding to either take a seat or leave the room, and go on reading from the Angelou essay. When I've finished the passage I look up and see the two young women have now taken seats. One combs her hair; the other, head on hand, stares blankly at the window. I ask the latter if she needs to see the school nurse. She nods and says, "I think maybe I swallowed a cockroach or something."

I stare at her for a moment, looking at the slightly swollen face, the tired eyes, the listless hands. I pick her up and carry her out of the classroom. She's surprisingly light in my arms, as if her bones were hollow. I go down the hall about thirty feet to a door left ajar. I put her down in a pile of sawdust the janitor must use for sweeping the halls, and I pull over her the janitor's coat, covering her head. She must not awaken until students and teachers depart, until books close and go dumb, until halls and classrooms bristle with silence.

Insomnia of the News

Waking, you bump into the television.
Orange striped fish sleepily float
in and out of view. On every channel,
orange striped fish. Yawning,
you wait for a commercial to explain
what to do. A man in a white asbestos suit
sprays his home with fire. "Do it now," he warns,
"before they do."

        Beneath the door, water
feels its way. Fish gently pass, back
and forth, through a woman's puffy face.
I can't sleep, she sighs. "If I sleep
they'll come, and steal my baby."
"Have you thought about a chocolate laxative?"
the tv doctor muses. Orange-striped fish nibble
the wall of the woman's mouth.

        Outside,
where it's raining, it rains. Trash fires burn
the rain, and the rain burns
the fire. A homeless man, holding out
a cardboard sign, slows a pedestrian.
The passerby shakes his heavy head. It must be
a kind of blessing.

        An orange striped fish swims
through your right eye. "Come in," you say,
"I've been expecting you."

SCIENCE AS A MECHANISM

To Dance with Uranium

Uranium islands shadow the side of the hill.
There is no hill unworthy of our love.
There is no hill that is not home to someone.

If I were not dancing with uranium, would you dance with me?
You could dance with me wearing forks and spoons.

My dance tells of fields and streets and homes
no one can live in.
My dance tells of rivers flowing in five directions.
Uranium gives me this power to dance
without ever tiring.

What has a hole in the side of a word
got to do with what the word says?
What has the word "uranium"
got to do with uranium?
How can a word ever take us
to the place where the word ends its conjuring?

At last, uranium will embrace you
just as you have invited it to.
At last, you will know what it is to dance
long after your body has stopped dancing.
This is not magic.
This is a dance you already know the steps to.

I draw a circle on the ground
so everything I say will be contained and not harm you.
One day the circle will break.
This is not magic.
It is the dance with uranium that awaits you.

Radithor: A Short History in Four Reels

"Our ignorance is profound."
—Scott Russell Sanders

Reel 1

When Eben MacBurney Byers tumbled out of the top berth of his private Pullman compartment ("She was worth it," he told the porter, slipping him a cigar), he knew exactly what to do. Make those sitting in the cinematic dark forget they were sitting in the cinematic dark. Despite the injured arm, the bruised groin, the gouged tongue: Deadpan. Deader than any ever delivered by that cretin Buster Keaton. It worked. They applauded Eben Byers, not because he was chairman of A. M. Byers Steel, a director of Westinghouse Electric & Manufacturing, golf champion, horse race enthusiast, ladies' man extraordinaire. No, they applauded his raw athleticism, his vulnerable indestructibility, his compassionate indifference to fate.

Reel 2

He had lost that pep, that zip, that pizazz, he told his physiotherapist. Since the fall from the Pullman berth, he didn't care about the Harvard-Yale game. Hell, he didn't even want to sue Pullman. And the ladies were whispering unkindnesses about his private performances. Radithor, said Dr. Macklis. Radithor, said Mr. William J. A. Bailey, entrepreneur, who promised that "this new weapon of medical science would improve the blood supply sent to the pelvic regions, infusing depleted organs with energy." Cure for 156 maladies. Byers drank two or three bottles a day. "The radium knows just what to do," Byers bragged to his business partners. He sent cases of Radithor to Carnegie, to the Fitzgeralds, to W.C. Fields. He had it served in stainless steel goblets at the Kentucky Derby to his race horses. The cinematic darkness roared.

Reel 3

More than 1,400 half-ounce bottles of the elixir later, something was wrong. Headaches, loss of weight, teeth falling out. Byers complained to his doctors that he'd lost "that toned-up feeling." Asked to testify at Federal Trade Commission hearings on Radithor, Byers declined—he found he couldn't raise his body from the bed. For the sake of posterity, he flashed (head propped up on pneumatic pillows) his deadly deadpan. "Famously, he did not smile," noted the New York Times. Nervous titters in the cinematic darkness. After the photographers filed out, Byers rasped to an assistant, "Get a case of Radithor off to that fairy Keaton, now."

Reel 4

Bone tissue disintegrating. Holes forming in the skull. Byers' upper jaw, excepting two front teeth, and his lower jaw had to be removed. 156 maladies. Silence in the cinematic dark. The FTC paid a visit to one William J. A. Bailey. Health stores removed Radithor from their shelves. In Pittsburgh, rumors of a lady friend of Byers dying of a mysterious ailment. March 31, 1932, Byers wired Keaton: "You win." At age 51, Eben MacBurney Byers fixed his final deadpan. "Mr. Keaton," reported *The New York Times*, "could not be reached for comment." "Radium will do," muttered the medical examiner at the autopsy, "what radium will do."

Watch Alice Glow

"Sometimes we'd get the neighborhood kids to watch Alice glow
in a dark closet. They'd get a good laugh out of that."
—Claudia Clark, *Radium Girls: Women and Industrial
Health Reform,1910-1935*

Creeping and slithering on their bellies in no man's land
doughboys find the pocket watch too clumsy. Wrist watches

are the weapon of choice. Soon wrist watch dials glow
on the battlefield and at the homefront. Glow in dark

industrial magic. Factories employ young women, for dial painting
is clearly "women's work." Midteens to early twenties, white, single,

newly married, childless. Easy work. Good wages. Inevitable.

*

Back bent
to task
she sits, long
skirt well below
her knees, lean
legs tucked
beneath wooden
chair, one dial painter
looking remarkably
like the others
all the way along
the long workbench.

"The women applied radium to their buttons, their fingernails,
their eyelids, at least one coated her teeth with it

before a date, for a smile that glowed in the dark. At night
their fingers glowed, their hair shone in the dark."

The young woman
closest to us touches
her paintbrush tip
to her tongue
to sharpen the point
for the application
of radium, a cup
of which is generously
proffered her by
a silent assistant,
a skeleton, one
kindly attending each
of the comely
young dial painters.

*

Radium water, claim researchers,
is "known to stimulate
the blossoming of lilac buds
and accelerate growth
of tadpoles."

*

The radium-rich waters of the Hot Springs National Park,
"may reasonably be expected," proclaims the National Park Service
in 1907, "to give relief in the following conditions":

in gout or rheumatism
in neuralgia
in the early stages of chronic Bright's disease

in catarrhal conditions of the gall bladder
in certain forms of disease of the pelvic regions
      and in sterility in women
in chronic malaria, alcoholism, drug addictions
in many chronic skin diseases
in some forms of anemia
in syphilis
in gonorrheal rheumatism
in toxemia and conditions of defective elimination
in some forms of cardiovascular disease
in conditions of debility and neurasthenia.

*

"Is it, then, any wonder
that we regard radioactivity
as an unknown god?"

*

"It was in November 1923 I begin to have trouble
with my teeth," notes Katherine Schaub, a dial painter.

"My dentist advised that I have two teeth extracted.
After the teeth were taken out, I continued to go

to the dentist for treatment, but failed to get any relief
from the pain. I kept seeing teeth glowing in the dark.

I cannot explain why, but I did."

*

From *The Book of the Radioactive Dead*:
Irene Rudulf
Hazel Vincent Kuser

Amelia Maggia
Helen Quinlan
Marguerite Carlough

*

Syphilis, phosphorus poisoning, anemia,
trench mouth, pneumonia, necrosis of jaw, and septicemia.
Such are the official causes of death for dial painters.
Anything but a reference to a brush dipped in radium
placed between the lips to make a fine tip.

*

Harrison Martland kept a notebook listing the names
of all dial painters. Each time a dial painter died, the medical examiner

recorded a red "D" beside the name, notes *Life* magazine
below a photo of Martland, pencil poised over his open ledger,

mouth slightly agape, surrounded by his bone samples in glass jars.
"Radium Poisoning Radiation Osteitis Spine McDonald," says one label

for our scientific edification. If it hadn't been for those dial painters,
notes a Manhattan Project manager, there would have been no

remote control gadgetry, no dust-dispersal systems, no filtering
of exhaust air for the builders of the first atomic bombs.

*

"The hair, faces, hands, arms, necks,
the dresses, the underclothes, even the corsets
of the dial painters luminous."

*

"So many of the girls I know won't own up," says Katherine Schaub
of her fellow dial painters. "They say they are all right. They're afraid

of losing their boyfriends and the good times. Afraid of being
ostracized. They know it isn't rheumatism that makes them limp."

*

"There recently have been rumors and comments
made by individuals," the U.S. Radium Corporation informs
its workers in 1924, "in which they claim work
in our application department is hazardous
and has caused injury and poor health
to a former operator of ours and they are advising that other
of our operators should discontinue being in our employ.

We do not recognize that there is any such hazard
in the occupation."

*

One dial painter had undergone twenty operations
on her jaw and then developed discharging ulcers
under her chin; damage to her spinal cord
had also paralyzed her legs. "Poor
personal hygiene," said U.S. Radium.

*

"We were only girls," says Schaub, "15, 17, 19 years old."

*

From *The Book of the Radioactive Dead*:
Elizabeth Dunn
Helen Wall
Marjorie Dumschott
Frances Splettstockher
Mildred Demolis

*

Orange, New Jersey dentist Joseph Knef offers U.S. Radium
a deal: If the firm hires him, he'll treat all of its injured dial painters

and keep quiet about the causes of the illnesses and urge the "girls"
not to file suits: "I'll keep my mouth shut. I will use my influence.

Do you want me as a friend or do you want me as an enemy?"
The company calls his offer "immoral" and sends women detectives

posing as dial painters to Dr. Knef. He has them strip to their waists
(without a nurse present) and finds no sign of jaw necrosis.

But he tells the young women to sue U.S. Radium. He will supply
the proof, he tells them. "An expert," the doctor explains,

"always testifies on the side that is paying him."

*

From *The Book of the Radioactive Dead*:
Margaret Looney
Ella Cruse
Inez Vallat
Genevieve Smith
Josephine Smith

Jennie Stocker
Eleanor Eckert
Louise Pine

*

"I was told that my limping condition was causing talk
and it wasn't giving a very good impression of the company

and they felt it was their duty to let me go," says Catherine Donahue
fired in 1931 by Radium Dial in Ottawa, Illinois. Seventy-one pounds

and "dying by inches," Donahue succumbs in 1938 to radium poisoning.
On the day after her death, Radium Dial files an appeal of her award.

In the factory, the supervisor tells the dial painters nothing is wrong
with the women, nothing is wrong with radium.

*

From *The Book of the Radioactive Dead*:
Katherine Schaub
Catherine Donahue
Anna Stasi
Irene Colby LaPorte
Ana Mullenite
Florence Koss
Katherine Moore
Ethel Daniels
Sarah Carlough Maillefer
Mabel Adkins
Edith Lapiana

"None of us under any circumstances
care to carry on the work," says Howard Barker,
the president of U.S. Radium in 1931,
"if we felt that by doing so
we were unduly jeopardizing the health
of those employed in the industry."

*

In 1978, dial painters notice their calluses glow in the dark.
"Sometimes I'd get up at night and look in the mirror

and my hair would be glowing," says Pearl Schott
decades after the first dial painters glowed. "Don't worry about it,"

says a luminous official when Schott asks about her massive
gastrointestinal bleeding. "Lots of people have that,"

her foreman tells her. "Nothing is wrong."

*

"We wonder," wonders C.W. Wallhausen,
Vice President of U.S. Radium, "if the public
has enough of an understanding of radioactivity
to properly use such information
and not become even more confused
than it is now."

*

With ten thousand dollars and one year to live, former dial painter
Katherine Schaub: helps with her parents' mortgage,

buys a coat and tan felt hat to match, as well as four silk dresses,
a white flannel sport shirt, a rose-colored sweater, two silk blouses,

lingerie, stockings, shoes, and a purse. She also buys an automobile,
goes to a rural health resort, takes some correspondence classes,

and works on her autobiography, which her parents destroy
after her death. "While other girls are going to dances and the theater

and courting and marrying for love," she notes, "I remain here
and watch death approach." In 1930, all her money gone,

the newspapers grow suspicious of her for not dying
in the allotted year. Schaub stumbles up a stair. Bone

above the knee fractured. Radium's sweet kiss.
Cancer of the bone. Schaub refuses to allow

amputation of her leg. On February 18, 1933,
she dies at age 30 and is buried in the Holy Sepulcher Cemetery,

Newark, New Jersey. Her febrile bones glowing
like watch dials she once painted. Watch Katherine glow.

*

From *The Book of the Radioactive Dead*:

"And burn me, O Lord, with a fiery zeal
Of thee and thy house, which doth in eating heal."

*

When closing the Luminous Process plant in Ottawa, Illinois,
in the early 1980s, the owners perform one last gesture

of human kindness—they donate thirty-five dial painting desks
to a local Catholic school. After the desks were discovered

to be radioactive, the firm was forced to take them back.
See you in *The Book of the Radioactive Dead.*

They'd get a good laugh out of that.

Sailors Shielding Their Eyes
During Atomic Bomb Test, Bikini, 1947

Light,
unbearable
light

Is what moves
your head
into the crook of your arm,
slides your other arm
across your chest
in a tight
half-embrace.

Face buried, eyes
shut, you can see
someone in white,
years from now,
with a knife too sharp
to feel, slicing
along your testicles.

Will the seed
you carry be able to spawn
a child
impervious to the might
you witnessed, back
at Bikini?

Or did the flash
bloom a cancer
there in the darkness
of your scrotum?

You strain to hear
the words of the doctor—
"It's a blessing,"
he tells you. Or does he say—
"It's for the best"?

You press your head
deeper
into the crook of your arm.

I Sing the Body Atomic

"[M]y parents were ordinary people . . . ."
—Robert Meeropol, "Rosenberg Realities"

We are all children of the atomic bomb. I was only two months
past my third birthday when my father was arrested in 1950.

The electric chair, invented by Thomas Edison in the mid-1880's,
has its origins as a human reform of capital punishment. "Hoover

sent me," said one spy to the other. An F.B.I. man turned off
the radio. Bandits were trying to frame the Lone Ranger. I turned

it on: he turned it off again. Well-known Pittsburgh industrialist
Eben Byers drank a bottle a day of Radiothor, an expensive radium

tonic, from 1926 until 1931, when he contracted cancer of the jaw.
It unmanned him. "Roy Cohn is not a homosexual," said Roy Cohn;

"Roy Cohn is a heterosexual man who fucks around with guys."
"Have you no sense of decency, sir, at long last?" McCarthy sent Cohn

around the country electrocuting dogs and cats in public
demonstrations. I don't know what animals I am dealing with,

but I know I'm dealing with animals. My brother asked a guard
if he could see the electric chair and did not cry. Jell-O again.

"Should Michael ask. . . answer briefly," Ethel adds in another letter,
"that it is painless electrocution." "I sing Peat Bog Soldiers, United

Nations, Tennessee Waltz, Irene, Down in the Valley, Beethoven's
Ninth," writes Julius; "I feel good and strong when I sing."

And there appeared unto them cloven tongues like as of fire,
and it sat upon each of them. "The age of innocence is dead,"

announced Fiedler. In Georgia, the Pyatigorsk Superior Radon Center
still prepares radon drinks, baths, enemas, vaginal and nasal

irrigations for more than one thousand patients per day. That
scrawny cry. A pornographic plume of smoke rising from Ethel's

head. "Her dowdy head," notes Fiedler. History has been banished.
Tomorrowland, atomic spies, the electronic chair. The line between

private and public, between fact and fiction broken down. Nothing
is what it seems. Ethel sent me. Julius sent me. Walt sent me.

I sing the body atomic. The atomic bomb is fiction. The Rosenbergs
a fiction. We remain, all of us, children of the atomic fiction.

This is why I'm not bitter.

After Viewing *The Queen of Outer Space* (1958)

One of those films
so bad you can't forget—
a planet of nubile women
in skimpy skirts and heels,
armed with caulking guns.

And the Queen of Outer Space—
a white mask
with loopy gold wires
at the top, quivering
whenever she spoke.

Yet her mask couldn't disguise
or make humorous the fact
that men
with an atomic bomb
forever scarred her face.

For that, she'll destroy
these men from Earth
and the Earth itself.
But for one kiss
from the handsome captain,

one kiss on a face
only one of the damned
could understand.
I think of those women,
Hiroshima Maidens,

whose faces bore
the signature of the Bomb
thirteen years before

this film was released.
I think of Hiroko,

one of the chosen,
saying of a face
surgeons couldn't heal:
"Like when you tear your dress,
patches is patches."

Twenty-nine operations later,
and the skin
on her chin too smooth,
puffy: "This is my stomach
skin, that's why

getting too fat. But
I don't like to trouble
any more." Arthritis
in her right elbow,
left arm stiff

from that August morning
when history burned
into bone, Hiroko says,
"If I think back
on my life, I think,

I was really a lucky girl."
Such luck
I cannot imagine.
There are some scars
even a kiss cannot erase.

Rapture of Fire: Amarillo, Texas, 1984

"Then two shall be in the field; the one shall be taken,
and the other left."
                                        —Matthew 24:40

My friends,
if the Bomb drops
on Amarillo today,
it won't bother me one bit.
For when the trump of God sounds

We'll be traveling
186,000 miles a second!
We'll sing like a meteor!
Raptured right up in the firmament
above Amarillo.

Why don't you do it tonight,
Jesus? Do it tonight!
Oh, that would be fantastic.
If you're ready to go,
it would be fantastic.

When rockets take off,
they leave a trail of fire.
When we leave this old earth,
we're going to leave a trail
of Holy Ghost fire.

We'll look back down
on the houses where we lived
and we'll say: "Goodbye,
You piece of junk!
Goodbye, old shack!"

Oh yes, and then pretty soon
we'll be seeing the lights
of Dallas, and the lights
of Houston, and in the west
the lights of Los Angeles.

And we'll say, "Goodbye,
Dallas! Goodbye, Houston!
Goodbye, devouring fire! Goodbye!"

Escalation

And the escalators go down and down, row upon row of escalators,

the light so bright, the surfaces shining so, it hurts, to go down and down,
the light so slow. All motion a descending descent, me in my avocado

paper suit, with a hood that won't close, to protect me from the breath
of radiation, the warning siren going off with its slow imitation
of a warning siren, I ride the escalators down, my cat in my arms, down,

wherever that is, the only direction left to go, though we could go down

faster, if there was some reason. Children I am to look after, somewhere
ahead, disappear, children who run down escalators, the light so bright,

I can't see where they've gone, children in their avocado paper suits,
hoods that won't quite stay closed, the breath of radiation so like ours, so
much like escalators, going down, never hesitating, into the world below,

where all breaths draw the same breath, over and over. Safe in the space

below the space where we are not safe, we continue to go down
on escalators that carry us to the only place an escalator can, to a small

landing, one two three steps, followed by another escalator, and another,
down, wherever that goes, the only direction to protect us, the light so bright,
the escalators, wherever they must go, go down, row upon row, down.

Science as a Mechanism of Exclusion

" [S]cientific discourse can be used as a mechanism of exclusion,
particularly when it is marshaled against anecdotal evidence . . . ."
—Valerie Kuletz, *The Tainted Desert*

At the top of the stairs the monster
      disguised as father
rears back and roars

      I stumble back to see
my sister flying off
      the edge of the knowable world

through the space
      between railing and stairframe
between collective

      and personal guilt
headfirst
      into family history

striking battleship gray
      concrete not nearly as hard
as the Bradley in my sister's head.

                              *

Legs unable to run
as fast as my body
my sister and I
freefall down the wall
of sand tumbling
into Atlantic Ocean.
I can hear Marconi
casting out

from his shack
on this Cape Cod shore
his invisible waves
upon these visible
waters: *Where*
wast thou
when I laid
the foundations
of the earth?
Whereupon
are the foundations
thereof fastened?

*

A feathery shadow gliding
    down from the bank tower
        diving
upon shadowy black cat.

Howl
    and screech as cat and owl
        discourse on
science as a mechanism of exclusion.

At work, the Chicanos break
    into excited Spanish when I tell them
        my story. Why
all the excitement? I ask.

"Two *brujas*,"
    they tell me, "you saw
        two *brujas*
fighting."

Once, remembers Alberto,
    in Sweetwater, Texas,
        this black cat
was tossed into a fire

"And in the ashes
    what did we see?
        Si, the naked body
of a woman.

*

From the back of the City of Dekalb water bill:

not a notice of immediate hazard to water consumers

in drinking water for radium 226 and 228 has been

The maximum allowable concentration for radium, as

is five pico curies per liter of water. The City of Dekalb exceeds

from naturally occurring minerals found in the deep sandstones

A portion of the radium which is ingested remains in

the radium, because of its high energy, can cause damage to

may result in the development of bone cancer in a very small

the short-term risk is minimal and no special precautions

Three a.m. custodial break, the shy
backwoods Arkansas couple, to pass the time
tell a story.

       A strange mechanical noise
off in the woods one night where no factories toiled.
They decide to walk the dog over
in that direction. The dog growls, backs
away, barking, runs home.

            A few minutes later,
the couple returns, enters the house, just a few
minutes later to watch t.v. Something is missing.
The show that was just coming on is over.
Two hours they cannot account for.
All they can remember—going off to the woods
and that strange unaccountable noise.

              A moment
of silence in the break room. Then back we go
to scrubbing the starry toilets. *Canst thou bind*
the sweet influences of the Pleiades, or loose
the bands of Orion?

*

The public relations man from the Idaho
National Engineering Lab is not a public relations
man from an engineering lab that uses the word
"engineering" to avoid the word "nuclear."
Think of him as your favorite science teacher, sixth
grade, and he is showing the class a slide show:
"Our Friend the Atom."

A person living
for an entire year right at the fence of a nuclear
power plant would receive less than one
millirem of radiation, about the same
an airline passenger receives flying
from Chicago to Los Angeles.

And:
one acquires this natural energy sleeping
alongside the radiation-bearing bones
of a lover.

Why, I wonder, is the woman
who lost her mother to cancer from radioactivity
released by naturally occurring nuclear
bomb blasts in Nevada, why is she blocking
all of us in the conference room
by sitting in the doorway?
Afterward
in the conference gift shop
amid arrowhead bolos and laminated elk dung
she releases the natural question
that will not give her rest:

"Where
in all this talk
maximum allowable concentration
less than one millirem
short-term minimal risk
where is the heart?"

*

White jeep, crowned with orange emergency
flasher, rusting snow blade
sheltering weeds

from the city grounds crew
                    driver's door ajar
inviting the passerby to have a sit
                    try to imagine:

Here, here is the site of the first Ottawa, Illinois
radium watch dial factory
                    now radioactive parking lot
with radioactive used cars and trucks.
                    There were no
and there are no cities
                    called Hiroshima and Nagasaki
only naturally occurring minerals
                    in the deep sandstones
only parking lots
                    used cars and trucks at
everyday naturally-occurring low prices.

                    *

Whereupon
are the foundations
thereof fastened?

                    *

In the garage how quickly grows
                    spider web
connecting lawnmower
    handle to tomato plant
                    wire mesh to folding
            table to bag of weed
killer to barbecue lid
                    handle to
        the blistered fingers of Madame Curie to

glowing radium-painted teeth
                    of Ottawa watch dial painters
to there are no and there were no cities
                    called Hiroshima
and Nagasaki
        to naturally-occurring radium in deep sandstones
how strong
        how fragile the anecdotal strands
trailing off
        behind me.

                        *

Rolling down two-lane blacktop
                    unable to see
anything except for the lights of Fort Collins
miles ahead of me
                    I know the road
is there because the road is there under me
The bicycle thump-thumps
                    over what
poor creature?
        Cat? Rat? Small dog?

I circle back in moonless darkness, unable to see
whatever is or was there.
                    The next morning in the building
where I parked my bicycle overnight
for the custodial graveyard shift
someone says, "A skunk
                    must have gotten in here
last night."
        Nodding, I wheel my skunk-
juiced bicycle away.
                    Guilty of rolling crimes.
Unscientific scientific chain reactions.

*

Square plastic wastebasket
at the top
          of the turning stairs
so boarding bus passenger
sees waste and basket and thinks:
This is not a flying vehicle
                              but a living
room with padded chairs and flashing
windows all mounted on a platform
balanced upon round gravity-bound wheels

coursing
     whether we admit it or not
between coursing atoms.

*

At the end of the driveway, back wheel
poised over the puddle by training wheels
I pedal with mechanical surety, not moving
the bicycle, but turning
                              my parents
brother and sister
                         a girl across the street
named Christy McAuliffe
                              Framingham
     Massachusetts
the clouds
          O there are and there are not cities
called Hiroshima and Nagasaki
                              this wheel-weary planet
turning in
          blessed-be-the-unfastened-
reach-of-unknowable-stars
                         circular wonder.

Story with Blue and Green

This is the story a child once told me. A child whose body
was crayon green, crayon blue, crayon green. The colors changed
back and forth with each step, sometimes even when he didn't
take a step. He stood in a field, a swirl of green and blue and green.

You might think with so much green and blue about, it would be hard
for him to know exactly what was the boy and what was the field,
but he knew. Every time he moved, he knew.

There were flowers, yellow balloon flowers. They bobbed,
though the boy couldn't feel a breeze. Maybe it's a slow breeze,
the boy thought, a breeze so soft and slow it moves through me,
back and forth, and I can't feel it. A you-can't-feel-me-but-I-can-
feel-you sort of breeze. The breeze moved through the boy
and the boy moved through the flowers, and the flowers
rubbed against the boy. He blushed yellow green and yellow blue.

Just then, he looked up. He couldn't say why. Maybe the soft,
slow breeze tilted his chin back. Maybe he heard a china cloud
breaking into smaller pieces of china clouds. Maybe someone
had told him, before he came here, before he knew
what he had to do: "After the yellow flowers, look up into the sky."

He saw it, watched as it got bigger, watched as it came nearer,
the falling bomb taking the shape of a falling bomb. His legs
knew what to do. Crayon blue and crayon green, they moved
through the blue green field. With each step he was more sure
that he could do it. He stretched his arms out to catch it,
the way he would catch a baby, falling out of the sky.

Perhaps he called out, "I got it!" But this is not a work of history.
In this story, the field is always green and blue, the bomb
always falling, the boy running, cradled arms always ready.

EARTH ANGEL

Earth Angel

1.
At the Colorado/Wyoming border
　　rising over the side of the road, shaggy
head and humped back saying: "buffalo"

white breath escaping open
　　mouth and nostrils, fugitive from what
sleeper's dream, there at the edge

of prairie and interstate.

2.
On the sign that read
　　"CAMPSTOOL"
perched the meadowlark

supporting the weightless Wyoming sky.

3.
Western Nebraska
　　or was it eastern Wyoming
spring green grass

in the long tracks
　　to the still windmill.

4.
Outside Chicago
　　on the door
of a dumptruck lit

by yellow dust—
　　"EARTH ANGEL."

The Institute of Nuclear Poetics

Before I was an institute, I grew tomatoes behind the garage.
Now I grow tomatoes and deduct all the expenses.

I share an office to help pay the rent. When the phone rings
I hear Dr. Strangelove on the calliope playing "Oh When the Saints."

A client from Sierra Blanca calls for a haiku to keep away
a nuclear waste storage facility. We laugh a low-level laugh.

When there's a lull, I read Kenneth Rexroth love poems
to the philodendron. The sandwich on my desk eavesdrops.

With each line I write, I pull the world back a little
from the edge. No wonder I sit and stare out the window.

The city owns my trees; I own the leaves. Is a maple ever homeless
no matter how far from Utica, or Omaha, or Cassiopeia?

I open the window and release another fool fly from captivity.
Has your hand ever tingled awake while you were asleep?

It's the silt of the century's confusion that collects, daily, nightly
on the windowsill. Some of it, too much of it, mine.

Animal Light

For Federico García Lorca

In the animal light
of May going into June
I ask you, Federico, who
died in your trousers?
Your cuffs? Your
sexual lint? The angel
of dust laughs
with her mortar and pestle.
How bone envies red
earth and red earth
bone. Even on the unmarked road
you never gnawed the flesh
of the sky in your flesh.
Because nothing is too beautiful
for the olive tree, you said.

The granddaughter
of the man who shot you—
rough red hair, green
eyes, purple lace-trimmed
socks. She sweeps
her kitchen floor into a cone
of paper, pours the dust
into the fire. Somewhere
below her feet, a boulder
turns. Its elemental speech:
cut and score, pit and groove.
The angel of the abdomen
works in her now. Works
with infinite tenderness,
infinite zeal.

Jesus and the Corn Mothers

Fray Tomás Carrasco and a group of Franciscans were preaching to some Pueblo women under a clear, untroubled sky. They berated the Indians with their usual complaint: the evils of the flesh. Fathers with daughters, brothers with sisters, mothers with sons. Only Jesus, only monogamy, only the missionary position could save the Pueblo. One of the Pueblo women, elderly but of good health, removed her clothing and stood naked before the friars. The other women sang:

> I am glad I have seen your nakedness.
> It is beautiful.
> Now it will begin to rain.

What happened next, all present, friars and Indians, agreed upon— a crooked stalk of lightning struck the Indian woman who had made herself naked before the friars.

"Can't you see," said Fray Carrasco, trying his best not to gloat exceedingly, "God struck the witch dead."

"Can't you see," said the Pueblo women, "the sky spirits called the woman to live with them as a cloud."

My Brother Calls from Cleveland (To Tell Me This Dream)

Here he is again, in the unfinished attic of the old wooden house where dreams end and begin. Someone has thrown open the trapdoor to the widow's walk so all that separates above from below is a thin blue membrane. My brother starts to sleepwalk up the long, paint-mottled ladder. Hands grab and flail. Mother and father, sister and brother grab hold of his arm, pull on his leg, tug on a shoe. His body cannot be stopped. Soon he's out of reach.

Climbing out of the trapdoor, he rises onto the roof, steps onto the shaky widow's walk railing, and, perched there, inhales the thin ethers of oblivion. Pushing off with his toes, his body flies free of the old house. For a moment, there's no more struggle. The wind eases past his face, strokes his hair, teases him with an earthen song he's sure he heard before:

"Rest your head, little brother, under the boughs of the dogwood tree. There's no place you don't belong. The kingdom above shall not be as the kingdom below. Rest your head, little brother, on the cool soil beneath the dogwood. There's no place else you need go."

Nothing can go wrong now. But something is wrong. Instead of falling, he's floating. His body glides of its own accord. Chest first, he lands smoothly on the damp front lawn. Once more. He must go back. Fight his way up the long wooden ladder. Throw himself off the roof. Again and again. Until he gets it right. Until he can finally rest.

"Rest your head, little brother. In the cool soil beneath the sleepy dogwood."

Letter to Dina

For Dina Mironovna Pronicheva, survivor of Babi Yar

Why does it take so long

for a body to fall, longer, say, than a long strand
of summer grain, blond as a blond soldier, a pinprick
of well water clinging to its side. Why is it, even as you fell,
a voice insisted: "This is the way to Palestine. This is the way out of
Kiev," down the wagon-rut scars cut into the face of the Black
Madonna, the way to the promised promised land.

No one told you

to jump, but you did, before the machine gun could grope
behind your breasts for your heart, and falling, you saw geese
fleeing northeast, children on their backs, facing the wrong
way, clutching reins tied to the tail, forgetting they were
not arriving, but leaving. Perhaps it was best, you thought,
the children not having to see where they were being taken.

And for some

reason not understandable still, you forgave the icicle
scars down your flesh, the tall pines standing watch over
those women herded off by the soldiers, the faces that never
emerged from the woods. For how long did I soak you in kettle-boiled
water, before we could peel away the vest stuck to your ribs
like moss, before I could bring my lips to kiss you.

Wherever you ask

I shall kiss you, whether in front of grandmother's kitchen
icon, down in the trench grandfather dug for an air-raid

shelter, or before the notice ordering all Yids to Melnikovsky
and Dokturov, whether among the bodies, naked, hugging
each other in the ravine, or before the sentry, searching
your papers while you repeated, in Ukrainian and German,

I am not a Yid

though it made no difference in the end, for they took you
to the sand quarry, the same place your parents had gone,
who, even as they fell, prayed you were alive, Dina, so
a schoolboy, lifting a pencil, writing in his notebook
the words "Babi Yar," might hear, through layers of sand
and bone and sand, what can never be muffled, the sound
the balalaika will always make you hear—a body falling

Into the Yar.

Terrestrial Music/2

I want to sleep
  until we float
out of our skins
  catch
on the maple's
  wet leaves
dripping
  onto the sleepless earth.

Mortal Colors

Gray, white, brown scoured November sky. You were wearing a gray coat with round white circles, each one held by a tiny gold safety pin, trembling in the wind. The dog with the electronic collar silently racing to the end of the lawn, where the sensors lay buried out of sight. Halting to hurl his carnivorous cry. "Anger, like sex, is quite sexual," the dog said, translating for us motion into language. Into private prophecy. Gray, white, brown, the bristles in my elementary mustache. "Everything in the world exists to end in a book," my mustache said, translating color into urgency. Into shades of public privacy. You blew to me from the bare trees. Gray, white, brown lingual strips woven by wasps into wind-ravaged papyrus. "Everything you say will be used by someone or something to fashion the walls of a home," the wasp colors said, translating specificity into curve. Curve into nonbinding text. The book that declares without declaring itself the first and last book. You will be wearing a nightgown with a round hole, a little bigger than a host, just below your navel. Do I place there my eye or my tongue? Either way, you and I will be read. Everything comes to this. Gray, white, brown, that's why I let them roam your humming hair.

The Uses of Poetry

For Muriel Rukeyser

1.
Their granary
bucking back and forth
on the clothesline,

sparrows, made
reckless by the winter
wind, dodge and spin.

2.
Break it, break the snow's
cold curve smothering
the seed, and the seed

will melt one day
back into song, song back
into birds, birds back into seed.

3.
This morning, Muriel,
after writing these words,
I threw myself into the embrace

of subzero winds once more,
breaking free the seed
a poem broke loose in me.

White Footprints

To the front door and then
quietly turning away:
the mailman's white footprints.

The sound of August
in January: sizzling
salted ice on the front steps.

My father, dwarfed
by mountains of snow, comforting
my mother: "It's only water."

Those yellow stains
in the snow—you watch.
Come April, dandelions.

How winter loves
to brag: "Brown stalk, brown
stalk, morning glory's glory."

Her black boots sag
in the hallway—listless
without snow.

Me, the snow, the crow:
I threw my arms out
and the crow took wing.

On the Way to Mecca

For Malcolm

It was on the plane
to Jedda,
your hajj to Mecca,

when you saw it.
Side by side: white,
black, brown,

yellow, red. All
fellow pilgrims
on the same journey.

The flies on one
flesh no different
than the flies

on any other.
That's how I
remember you,

Malcolm,
how I want you
to be remembered,

not that image
in the eyes
of those three

men that Sunday
afternoon
at the Audubon.

Not that last
moment, your arms
outstretched,

with your calm,
"Let's cool it,
brothers,"

just before
the shotgun
claimed your heart.

No, you're still
on that flight
to Jedda,

the pock-marked
face of another
traveler resting

on your shoulder,
your kinky red
hair aflame

in the sun,
your beautiful
blood and brain

a part, at last,
of a larger
praising.

On Hearing a Recording of the Voice of Walt Whitman

This voice can crack
                    river rock
                            or mend broken bone.
This voice can mend river rock
                    or crack
                            mended bone.
This voice poured Lincoln
                    a glass
                            of elderberry wine.
This voice poured Lincoln
                    into the roots
                            of elder trees.
I can hear stars
                being born, stars dying
                        inside this voice.
I can hear lilacs
                laying claim
                        to the soil,
the soil
    laying claim to the lilacs
                  in this voice.
This voice churns
                with the nebulae
                        churning inside
every voice.
        This voice carries
                everyone
even those
        who do not believe
                  they are returning
back
    to the source
                of every voice.

After a Rain

After a rain
my tongue swells

with the salt
from your neck.

The brain
is as soft

after a rain
as the tomato

below the wind.
With each turn

of our breath
the soil roots

the onion's
cool flame.

This is how
the flesh

of your nipples
is the same

as the iris
after a rain.

Notes

"Where I Live" is in memory of William Stafford.

"Improper Disposal" is for Ellen Franklin.

"Insomnia of the News" is for Jay Griswold.

"To Dance with Uranium" is for James Grabill.

"Watch Alice Glow" is for Bill Witherup. All the quotations in this poem are from Claudia Clark's *Radium Girls: Women and Industrial Health Reform, 1910-1935.* Information is also drawn from Catherine Caufield's *Multiple Exposures: Chronicles of the Radiation Age.*

"I Sing the Body Atomic" is for Robert and Richard Meeropol and in memory of their birth parents.

"Rapture of Fire" is adapted from a minister's sermon as related by A.G. Mojtabai in her *Blesséd Assurance: At Home with the Bomb in Amarillo, Texas* and used with her kind permission.

"Science as a Mechanism of Exclusion" is for Valerie Kuletz and Terry Tempest Williams. The biblical passages are from the Book of Job.

"Chronicle of Jesus and the Corn Mothers" is for Joe Gastiger. The poem is based on an incident described in Ramón A. Gutiérrez's *When Jesus Came, the Corn Mothers Went Away.*

"My Brother Calls from Cleveland (To Tell Me This Dream)" is in memory of Dan.

"Letter to Dina" draws on testimony in *Babi Yar* by A. Anatoli (Kuznetsov).

"The Institute of Nuclear Poetics" is for David Romtvedt.

"Mortal Colors" and "After a Rain" are for Jana.

JOHN BRADLEY is the author of *Love-In-Idleness: The Poetry of Roberto Zingarello,* which won the Washington Prize. He is editor of *Atomic Ghost: Poets Respond to the Nuclear Age* (Coffee House) and *Learning to Glow: A Nuclear Reader* (Univ. of Arizona). He teaches writing at Northern Illinois University and lives in Dekalb, Illinois, with his wife, Jana, and cat, Luna.

CURBSTONE PRESS, INC.

is a nonprofit publishing house dedicated to literature that reflects a
commitment to social change, with an emphasis on contemporary writing
from Latino, Latin American and Vietnamese cultures. Curbstone presents
writers who give voice to the unheard in a language that goes beyond
denunciation to celebrate, honor and teach. Curbstone builds bridges
between its writers and the public – from inner-city to rural areas, colleges to
community centers, children to adults. Curbstone seeks out the highest
aesthetic expression of the dedication to human rights and intercultural
understanding: poetry, testimonies, novels, stories,
and children's books.

This mission requires more than just producing books. It requires ensuring
that as many people as possible learn about these books and read them. To
achieve this, a large portion of Curbstone's schedule is dedicated to
arranging tours and programs for its authors, working with public school
and university teachers to enrich curricula, reaching out to underserved
audiences by donating books and conducting readings and community
programs, and promoting discussion in the media. It is only through these
combined efforts that literature can truly make a difference.

Curbstone Press, like all nonprofit presses, depends on the support of
individuals, foundations, and government agencies to bring you, the reader,
works of literary merit and social significance which might not find a place
in profit-driven publishing channels, and to bring the authors and their
books into communities across the country. Our sincere thanks to the many
individuals, foundations, and government agencies who have recently
supported Curbstone's endeavors: Community Foundation of Northeast
Connecticut, Connecticut Commission on Culture & Tourism, State of
Connecticut Legislature, Greater Hartford Arts Council, Griffis Foundation,
Hartford Courant Foundation, Lannan Foundation, National Endowment
for the Arts, and the United Way of the Capital Area.

Please help to support Curbstone's efforts to present the diverse voices and
views that make our culture richer. Tax-deductible donations can be made
by check or credit card to:
Curbstone Press, 321 Jackson Street, Willimantic, CT 06226
phone: (860) 423-5110   fax: (860) 423-9242
www.curbstone.org